# How to Make Money in Stocks and Become a Successful Investor

## Learn To Trade Successfully And Build Your Knowledge Base Of The Markets

### PARSON JODY

**Copyright 2022. All Rights Reserved.**

This document provides exact and reliable information regarding the topic and issues covered. The publication is sold with the idea that the publisher is not required to render accounting, officially permitted, or otherwise qualified services. If advice is necessary, legal or professional, a practiced individual in the profession should be ordered.

From a Declaration of Principles which was accepted and approved equally by a Committee of the American Bar Association and a Committee of Publishers and Associations.

In no way is it legal to reproduce, duplicate, or transmit any part of this document in either electronic means or printed format. Recording of this publication is strictly prohibited, and any storage of this document is not allowed unless with written permission from the publisher. All rights reserved.

The information provided herein is stated to be truthful and consistent. Any liability, in terms of inattention or otherwise, by any usage or abuse of any policies, processes, or Instructions contained within is the solitary and utter responsibility of the recipient reader. Under no circumstances will any legal obligation or blame be held against the publisher for reparation, damages, or monetary loss due to the information herein, either directly or indirectly.

Respective authors own all copyrights not held by the publisher.

The information herein is offered for informational purposes solely and is universal as such. The presentation of the data is without a contract or any guarantee assurance.

# TABLE OF CONTENTS

## INTRODUCTION 5

### CHAPTER 1 7

**OPTIONS TRADING EXPLAINED 7**

### CHAPTER 2 20

**RISK AND OPTION PARAMETERS 20**

### CHAPTER 3 32

**UNDERSTANDING OPTIONS     PRICING 32**

### CHAPTER 4 39

**PLACING YOUR FIRST TRADE 39**

### CHAPTER 5 57

**STRATEGIES 57**

**TO CONSIDER 57**

### CHAPTER 6 68

**ANALYZING YOUR RESULTS 68**

### CHAPTER 7 75

**TIPS FOR SUCCESS 75**

# INTRODUCTION

Congratulations on purchasing this book, and thank you for doing so. As the name implies, this book will provide you with the foundation that you need to trade options successfully from the ground up. This means lots of examples and a focus on the basics to the exclusion of complicated concepts with the end goal of providing you everything you need to confidently head out and start making the types of trades that will help you to reach your goals.

To that end, the following chapters will discuss everything you need to know about options trading in order to engage in it successfully including things like, what options are, how they get their unique prices, how to know when you have found a good potential trade and actually placing a trade using one of the best platforms for beginners available.

Additionally, you will find a number of starting strategies to consider as well as ways to ensure your success and to know you are moving in the right direction.

There are plenty of books on this subject on the market, thanks again for choosing this one! Every effort was made to ensure it is full of as much useful information as possible, please enjoy!

# Chapter 1

## OPTIONS TRADING EXPLAINED

At their most basic, options are a type of security that can be traded, in much the same way as more traditional stocks and bonds. Essentially, when you purchase an option you are purchasing a contract that gives you the ability to either buy or sell a specific type of asset at a certain price for a certain period of time. While this may seem complicated, in reality, it is much the same process that anyone who has ever purchased a home via a loan has been through.

In this case, the buyer and the seller make an agreement for the price of the house and then the price of the house is confirmed, even if it takes a while for the process of obtaining a loan from the bank to be completed. In the interim the housing market could change in such a way that the price of the home has increased dramatically, which would be good for the buyer, or the price of the home could decrease significantly, at which time the buyer could withdraw their offer. Either way, the contract (or option) protects the buyer to ensure they get a specific deal regardless of what happens between the point the contract is agreed upon until its expiration date.

There are many different types of options, though this guide is going to focus largely on stock options, and they can all be broken down into two primary categories those that are calls or those that are puts.

*Calls:* When you are going to buy a specific option, this action is referred to as a call. When you call an option, you are doing so with the assumption that the underlying stock related to that option is going to increase in value before your call expires so you can sell the stock for a profit. If you exercise your company stock options, you are calling those options.

*Puts:* If you are selling a specific stock at a specific price you are instead creating a put option. In this instance you hope that the stock you are selling is going to decrease in price significantly before the option expires which is how you make money in this case. Puts are also often used by those who already own shares of a risky stock to protect their primary investment. Exotic options vary in many more ways and should not be considered until you are comfortable with everything vanilla options have to offer.

Furthermore, there are additional broad categories that all options, be they puts or calls, also fall into. The following are what are known as *vanilla options* which are those with specifications you are going to run into most often.

**American options:** Regardless of where it originates, an option is considered an American option if it can be acted upon at any point prior to its expiration time.

**European options:** Regardless of where it originates, an option is considered to be a European option if it can only be acted upon at the precise moment it expires.

**Short options:** An option with an expiration date of minutes, hours or days is said to be a short option

**Long options*:* Long options are those that do not expire for a year or more which makes them better suited for long term investing instead of daily trading. Long options are sometimes referred to as long equity anticipation securities or LEAPS.

Additionally, those who actively trade options

can be grouped into 4 categories, *holders* are those who buy options and those who sell them are referred to as *writers*. From there, holders and writers are broken down based on whether they work mostly in calls or mostly in puts. Of the pair, holders have more power than writers because they have a choice to either use an option to buy the related stock in question or to let the time run out on the option if the market didn't move in the way they expected. Writers, on the other hand, are limited in what they can do based on what the holder in question decides upon.

### Options Lingo

While there is little going on in an options exchange that is all that opaque, the amount of obscure sounding jargon that the average options trader can spew in under 30 seconds can make the process more intimidating than it ultimately needs to be. Do yourself a favor and become familiar with the following words and phrases and you'll be well on your way to sounding like a professional or at least not becoming lost in their conversations.

**Strike price:** The strike price is the starting price of the stock you are buying the option to purchase or sell depending if you are creating a call or a put.

**Exercise**: If the market moves in such a way that the amount of your strike price sounds appealing and you want to sell or buy the stock at the price in question then you are said to be exercising the option.

**Trading out**: If you as the holder agree to sell an option, the writer of that same option can then purchase it back in a process known as trading out. This is how more than 50 percent of all options trades end. Only 10 percent of options are ever fully exercised.

**Listed:** If an option is listed on a national exchange it is said to be listed. Listed options have clear strike prices as well as clear expiration dates which makes them a great place for new options traders to start. Listed options are most likely going to deal in 100 shares of stock of the related stock.

*Underlying stock:* The underlying stock of an option is the specific stock that the option is dealing in.

**In the money:** On a call, if the price of the underlying stock rises above the stock price then that option is said to be in the money.

**Intrinsic value:** When a call is in the money, the difference between the current price and the strike price is referred to as its intrinsic value.

**Time value:** How much time a specific option has until it expires is said to be its time vale.

***Volatility:*** If the underlying stock related to a particular option is prone to extreme fluctuations in price with little warning then it is said to have a high level of volatility.

***Premium:*** The total price of the option in question including a combination of stock price, strike price, time value and volatility.

**Primary uses for options investing**

Professional options investors utilize options in two main ways, to minimize the risk of other investments or to bet on the way the market is going to be heading in the near future. Betting on the market is referred to as speculation and options traders who can read the market can use it to make money regardless of the direction the market is heading in. Speculators need to know how the market is going to move but also the speed at which it is going to do so which is why speculation can be responsible for huge financial swings in both directions. The volatility comes from the fact that each option is 100 shares so relatively small movements in the underlying stock can lead to significant movement in related options.

While speculation can be risky, using options to hedge other investments is anything but. In this scenario, the options the trader purchases are essentially a type of insurance that protects other investments the trader has made. This is particularly helpful if another investment is a stock that has a high volatility as a put option will allow the trader to ensure they at least get their money back if the stock price of the underlying stock drops dramatically. Likewise, if the underlying stock dramatically increases in value then the trader can let the option expire and only be out the related fees paid on the options trade. This process means that traders can pursue risky but potentially profitable trades while protecting themselves as much as possible.

**Know what to expect**

If you are planning to trade successfully on a regular basis, the first thing you are going to need to work on is removing your emotions from the process completely. Your goal will be to create a trading plan (discussed in chapter 4) which you can stick to completely, which will make it easier for you to make the right choices even if several trades have not gone in your favor and your emotions are getting the better of you.

The first step in this process, however, is to have a realistic idea of just what to expect from your initial foray into options trading. This means getting rid of any flights of fancy that you might have that tell you that you will get rich after just a few trades and that you don't need to do any research and can instead rely on your gut to see the types of long term results you are looking for. Additionally, you will want to start by keeping a journal of the emotions you feel through each part of the trade in question so that you can look back on them later on and get a clear idea of when you are likely to experience what type of emotion and why.

As a general rule, the biggest cause for concern among new options traders stems from the fact that they expect things to always go according to plan. In fact, this is never going to be the case 100 percent of the time and even a tried and true system is never going to turn out perfect results, that's why investing in options is considered riskier than some other types of investing you might choose. You will find this fact easier to accept if, instead of focusing on whether or not each trade made money, you focus on following your system to the letter every time and not letting emotion or the results of the previous trades distract you from following through in the best way possible.

Successful options traders are those who follow their systems to the letter and let the fact that their system average is above 50 percent guarantee that they are going to make money in the long term. With this in mind, you will find it easier to deal with losing trades in the moment and also find it easier to choose reliable options trades over those that offer high margins for both risk and reward. This mindset will be easier to think about achieving than actually achieving and first, but it is important to keep in mind the fact that the longer you practice restraint, the easier it will be to practice it in the future.

## Chapter 2

## RISK AND OPTION PARAMETERS

When it comes to options trading, the various types of risk that come into play are referred to as one of the *Greeks.* Each variable is then given a different name and there are different ways to go about ensuring that each has as little of an effect on your trades as possible. Trading without first taking the time to clearly understand each of the Greeks and what they mean would be like driving in a foreign country where you were unfamiliar with the basic rules of the road or even the language the signs are written in.

When you look at placing a put or call on a specific underlying stock, or building your general options trading strategy, it is important to always consider the rewards and risks from three primary areas. The amount of price change, the amount of volatility change and the relevant amount of time value the option has left. For holders of calls, this risk can further be identified as either prices moving in the wrong direction, a decrease in volatility or there not being enough useful time left on the option in question. On the contrary, sellers face the risk of prices moving in the wrong direction and an increase in volatility but never when it comes to the time value.

When options are combined or traded, you will then want to determine the Greeks related to new result, often referred to as the *net Greeks.* This will allow you to determine the new difference between risk and reward and act appropriately. Understanding the various Greeks and what them mean will also allow you to tailor your strategy based on your own aversion to risk. Consider them as starter guideposts to ensure you are on the right track when it comes to seeking out the right options for you. There are numerous Greeks to consider and each are outlined in detail below:

**Delta**

When it comes to individual options, Delta can be seen as the amount of risk that currently exists that the price of the underlying stock is going to move. If the strike price of an option is the same as the current price of the underlying stock, then that stock can be said to have a Delta of .5. This can further be interpreted as meaning that if the underlying stock moves 1 point, the price of the option will shift .5 points assuming everything else remains the same. The total range Delta can possibly be anywhere from -1 to 1. Puts can be anywhere from -1 to 0 and calls can be anywhere from 0 to 1.

Delta is likely the first measurement of risk that you will always want to consider when it comes to choosing the options that are right for you. It is especially helpful when you are deciding when to buy a put option as you want it to be far enough from the current price to make a profit but not so far as to be unreasonable. In this instance, it is beneficial to know the expected results of paying less in exchange for knowing the Delta is going to be lower as well. This difference can be seen by simply looking at the strike price and watching how it changes in relation to the put price.

As a general rule, the less an option costs, the smaller its Delta is going to be. Delta is often linked to the odds that the option will be worth a profit by the time it expires. For example, if you are looking at an option with a Delta of .52, then you can generally assume, all other things being equal, that the option is slightly more likely than 50 percent to end favorably.

## Vega

When a position is taken, the risk of change that comes from the volatility of the underlying stock is referred to as the Vega. The level of volatility that an underlying stock has can change even if the price of the stock in question doesn't change; and regardless of the amount it changes, can affect the possibility of profits significantly. Successful strategies can be built around both low volatility and high volatility as well as neutral volatility in some cases. *Long volatility* options are those that increase in value as their amount of volatility goes up and *short volatility* is when value increases as volatility decreases. Strategies or trades that utilize long volatility are said to have a positive Vega and those that use short volatility are said to have a negative Vega. Options that have a neutral level of volatility can be said to have a neutral Vega as well.

As a general rule, the more time standing between an option and its expiration date, the higher that option's Vega is going to be. This is because time value is proportional to volatility as the longer the timeline, the greater the chance of volatility eventually happening will be. For example, if a certain $4 option's underlying stock is current trading around $90 with a Vega of .1 and a volatility of 20 percent. If the volatility increases just 1 percent that would be seen by an increase of 10 cents to a total of $4.10. If the volatility had instead decreased, the price of the $4 option would have decreased by 10 cents instead, leaving a total of $3.90. The amount of change that is seen in an option with a shorter period is often going to result in larger changes because there is ultimately less time the option will restabilize.

## Theta

Theta measure the rate at which the time the option has left is disappearing or decaying. This number is frequently going to be negative for your purposes. The moment you purchase an option, your Theta on that option begins decreasing which means the total value of the option begins to decrease as well because options are considered more valuable the longer the period of time they insure against new risk. If the amount of Delta on an option exceeds the Theta, then the option is considered profitable for the holder. If Theta instead exceeds the Delta, the profits go to the writer.

For example, if an option has a Thea of 0.015 then it is going to be worth 1.5 cents less tomorrow than it is right now. Puts have negative thetas and calls have positive thetas. This is because puts are worth the least when they are about to expire and calls are worth the most because the difference between the starting and ending amounts is going to be at its highest. Additionally, Theta fluctuates day to day as it starts off slow and then builds in intensity the closer the option gets to its ultimate expiration. This explains why long term options attract buyers and short term options are preferred by sellers.

If you are planning a trade that has the market remaining neutral then it is important to take Theta into account, but otherwise it is less likely to play into your strategy. Regardless, a general rule of thumb is to aim to purchase an option with the lowest Theta rate as possible.

**Gamma**

If Delta can be thought of as the amount of change that the option will experience when the underlying stock changes, then Gamma can be thought of as the measurement of how the Delta is likely going to change over time. Gamma increases as options near the point where the price of the option and the price of the underlying stock intersect and decreases the further below the strike price the price of the underlying stock drops. Larger Gammas are risky, but they also offer higher returns on average. Gamma is also likely to increase as a specific option nears its ultimate expiration date. This can be taken a step further with the Gamma of the Gamma which considers the rate the rate the Delta changes at.

For example, if a stock is trading at about $50 and a related option is currently going for $2. If it has a delta of .4 as well as a gamma of .1, then, if the stock increase by $1 then the delta will see an increase of 10 percent which is also the gamma amount. If volatility is low, then gamma is high when the option in question is above its strike price and low when it is below it. Gamma tends to stabilize when volatility is high and decrease when it is low.

**Rho**

Rho is the name for the risk relating to if the interest rates related to the option in question are going to change before its expiration. When it comes to choosing the system that is right for you Rho will be unlikely to factor into the equation in most instances. As interest rates increase, call prices will do the same while the price of puts will decrease and the reverse is true when interest rates decrease. Rho values are typically at their peak when the price of the underlying stock cross the price of the option in question. Likewise, this value is always going to be negative when it comes to puts and positive when it comes to calls. Rho values are more important when it comes to long options and virtually irrelevant for most short options.

**Find the Greeks**

When it comes to determining Greeks, it is important to keep in mind that most strategies will have either a negative or a positive value. For example, a positive Vega position will see gains when volatility rises and a negative Delta position will see a decrease when the underlying stock decreases. Keeping an eye on the Greeks and noting how they change is a key to options trading success in both the short and the long term.

When it comes to finding the Greeks for any option, the first thing you will want to keep in mind is that the results you get are always going to be theoretical, no matter how good they end up looking. They are simply projections based on a mathematical formula with various variables plugged in when needed. These include the bid you are putting on the option, the asking price, the last price, the volume and occasionally the interest. This information should then be plugged into the Greek calculator that your platform includes (as described in the next chapter).

# Chapter 3

## UNDERSTANDING OPTIONS PRICING

When it comes to trading options successfully, one of the first things you need to do is understand just how it is that options are assigned their relative value. Everything told, the price is made up of a combination of the expected dividends the underlying stock will produce, the interest rates, volatility, time value, intrinsic value and the current stock price. Of these, the volatility, time value, intrinsic value and current stock price play the largest minute to minute role in determining what you are going to pay for the options you purchase.

When it comes to deciding if a potential option is right for you, it is important to understand the difference between any premiums (profits) that the trade might generate and the theoretical value of the option in question. The premium is the amount the buyer is going to pay to get what is specific in the option as well as the money the seller will receive after they have written the option. By contrast, the theoretical value of an option is the amount the option should be worth based on all of the current market signs.

**Biggest influences**

*Current stock price:* When it comes to how the current stock price affects any related options, the two move as expected, though there is not a 1 to 1 correlation between them. In general, as prices rise, the price of calls will as increase and the price of puts will decrease and the reverse will occur if the price of the underlying stock is decreasing.

*Intrinsic Value:* The intrinsic value is the amount of value that the underlying stock is guaranteed to keep, even while the time value continues to decrease over time. To determine the intrinsic value of a call option you can either divide the underlying stocks current price by that price after the strike price of the related call has been subtracted from it. Conversely, you can find the intrinsic value of a put option by subtracting the price of the put from the current stock price and then dividing that result by the current stock price.

The result in either case will be a reflection of the type of advantage that exercising the option in question would generate. Essentially, it can be seen as the minimum amount you will get from the option. For example, if there is a company whose stock is currently selling at roughly $34.80 then a call option of $30 would intrinsically be valued at $4.80 because $34.80-$30=$4.80. If this were a put option, then it would have no intrinsic value because $30-$34.80=-

4.80 **and a negative intrinsic value is inherently 0.**

***Time Value****:* The time value is related to the amount of time an option has left and can more effectively be thought of as the likelihood with which it is going to exceed the amount of its intrinsic value. To determine the time value for any option you simply take the price of the option in question and then subtract the amount of its intrinsic value. As a rule of thumb, expect your options to lose around 30 percent of its value in the first 50 percent of its time on the market with the other 70 percent decreasing over the remainder of its time.

Continuing with the company with shares at $34.80 as discussed above, if the related contract is 30 days away from expiring and the related call option is currently going for $5 then the time value for the call is going to be set at 20 cents because $5 (the cost of the option) is subtracted from $4.80 (the intrinsic value). Alternatively, if the same stock was related to an option that is currently worth $6.85 that was not going to expire for 9 months then it would have a time value of $2.05 because $6.85 subtracted from $4.80 is $2.05. Regardless, the intrinsic value stays the same and the remainder of the price fluctuates based on the resulting time value.

The time value is also directly affect by the amount of volatility the stock in question is likely to experience in the time frame given. If the stock is expected to remain stable, the related time value cost would be low. The opposite is true for stocks with a high rate of volatility because the likelihood that they are going to change drastically before their expiration date is much greater.

***Volatility:*** While it is extremely important to measure correctly, volatility is the most subjective of all of the primary influences which can make it difficult to do so properly, especially for new options traders. Luckily there are several calculators that can be used to help successfully determine volatility. Additionally, there are numerous types of volatility, though historical and implied volatility are the two you should concern yourself with in the moment.

Historical volatility is the amount of volatility the underlying stock in question has seen in the past. It helps to illuminate potential future movements; specifically, how major they are likely going to be. Looking at the historical volatility will make it easier to determine the appropriate exercise price you will want to choose. Implied volatility is the amount of volatility the underlying stock has in the moment based on the current state of the market and relevant related prices. It can be used to help you accurately determine the potential of a possible trade.

# Chapter 4

## PLACING YOUR FIRST TRADE

Now that you hopefully have a clear idea of just what all the factors that go into making a good options trade are, it's time to start putting your new knowledge into action. This is a two-part process, the first part of which is coming up with the right plan and the second is executing on that plan in the right way.

**Work out a plan**

Before you can begin trading successfully, the first thing you are going to need to consider is creating your own personalized trading plan. This plan will include several facets that are unique to you and proceeding without taking the time to create your own plan is a good way to kill your options trading career before it starts.

*Start by considering your skills:* When it comes to ensuring you have the right options trading plan, the first thing you are going to want to do is take a look at your overall skill level and familiarity with trading in general, if not options trading specifically. Many new options traders are tempted to overestimate their skills early on, but this will do nothing but hold you back in the long run. Be honest and accurately catalogue your strengths and weaknesses. Specifically, you want to have a clear idea of how likely you are going to ignore your plan in favor of following your emotions. This is always a folly and if you know it is your tendency you are going to have to plan around it.

**Think about other challenges**: When it comes to determining what plan or system works for you, it will be important to take into account any other potential challenges that you might need to face in order to achieve the level of success that you are hoping for. These types of challenges could be anything from a lack of resources or planning to something more complicated and personal. The point is, anything outside of the normal market inconsistencies that prevent options trading from being purely profitable should be accounted for to ensure your success rate remains as high as possible.

*Consider the right amount of risk for you:* When it comes to deciding how much risk is the right amount for you, the first thing you are going to want to do is decide how much your total investment budget is going to be. If you have never invested anything before then this investment budget can be seen as your portfolio. A good rule of thumb is to never put more than 5 percent of your total into any one trade which makes it difficult to lose anything too substantial all at once. What's more, you are going to want to determine if the trade is worth the effort by ensuring it is going to pay off at least 300 percent when compared with the initial investment.

This is what is known as the risk/reward ratio and it can be found when it comes to any options trade by simply taking the amount of estimated profit and dividing it by the amount of the investment. If the result is greater than or equal to 3 the trade will be worth your time if it pays out. It is important to keep in mind that the return will only happen if the trade works in your favor, however, which can be determined by finding your own level of tolerance when it comes to investment risk.

Finding your own tolerance level when it comes to risk can be accomplished by taking the amount of time you have available to work on investing versus the amount of potential returns you are looking for. This means that the less time you are willing to spend on investing in options, the more risk you are going to have to be willing to accept if you are hoping to make more than a moderate amount of money from doing so.

***Do your homework:*** Each and every day in the hours before the market opens you need to plan on being in front of some type of screen, learning about everything that happened while you were sleeping and deciding how you think it is going to affect the markets you are interested in the most. This means checking foreign markets, the premarket forecast and the index futures to name a few, all in the name of deciding what the market's mood of the day is going to be after the day gets going properly and trading actually begins.

You will also want to always be aware of any

upcoming due dates for earning data to be reported which will always disrupt the market in question in one way or another. Companies have to report their earnings in comparison to their projections 4 times a year and the results are almost always going to affect the market in a serious way. The right choice in these instances is to wait until the rash of panic trading has passed and get in once things begin to stabilize but not so much so that there is no longer a profit to be made by doing so.

**Decide on an exit strategy:** No matter what plan or strategy you settle on, it is important to have a clear idea of what an acceptable level of profit or loss means to you and setting a firm exit strategy accordingly. While it can be tempting to wait on an underlying stock to rebound before exercise your option or walking away, the results are rarely going to end in your favor and it can lead to a bad habit of hanging on to sub-par trades that could possibly cost you big in the long term. The right exit strategy for you will vary based on how much risk you can accept, coupled with how many trades you are planning to make each day and what level of micromanaging you are comfortable with. Regardless, the point at which you decide to bail on a bad trade should be the same for all of your trades.

Setting up an effective exit strategy begins by deciding where the appropriate point to set what is known as a *stop loss* is. A stop loss is an automated order that you put in when you purchase the option which indicates at what point you want the option to automatically be sold. It is used to minimize your losses if a trade suddenly starts heading in the opposite direction you were hoping it would. You should avoid setting stop losses on options with extremely volatile because they are likely going to fluctuate too much to make them truly effective in this instance.

Stop orders are useful if you are the writer as well as the holder because they can be used to ensure that additional options are purchased if the price rises instead. You will also sometimes find it useful to use a secondary stop order which will sell if the price then hits a secondary amount. This is considered the *price target* and it is the amount that you can most expect to make on the trade in question. When you hit a price target you are going to want to sell off half of your total holdings and move the first stop point up to this point. This maximizes both your profit potential as well as minimizes your total risk.

For example, if you have a pair of options totaling 200 shares of a stock that is worth $20 to start. You would set a stop loss at $19.75 to prevent yourself from losing much money. If the stock then hits your price target of $30, then the best course of action is to sell 100 shares to ensure you see some profit from your price target before holding on to the remaining shares and setting a new stop loss of $30. This way you are guaranteed to see the profits of your previous price target while at the same time leaving yourself open for additional profits assuming the positive trend in the underlying stock continues.

**Find a point of entry:** Once you know when you are going to want to get while the getting is good, you will next want to determine when you are generally going to want to jump in on a profitable option trade. The best way to do this is to start by considering your acceptable risk and then decide what you want to do when you find an option that falls within your risk level. The most common entry decision is to buy a single option. Depending on your level of risk, you are also going to want to consider secondary factors, as you want your entry point to be discerning enough to weed out lousy propositions but no so stringent that the good ones also fail to get through. It will get easier to find the perfect entry point, the more practice you obtaining at trading options.

**Ask yourself about your goals:** When it comes to creating the type of trading system that is right for you, it is important to have a clear idea of just what you hope to accomplish when it comes to long term trading so you then have a better idea of how each individual trade can help you come one small step closer to your goals. You want to keep any limiting factors in mind when it comes to determining your goals, but you also want to keep your goals realistic as well as what is known as SMART.

*S:* The best goals are specific in that they make it clear why you want to reach the goal in question as which requirements stand in the way of your success. It will also make it clear when the goal is likely to be completed, where the completion will take place and who besides yourself you are going to need to call upon to complete it successfully. Specific goals are important because they are far more likely to be completed than those that are general.

*M:* The best goals are measurable which means they have several points that can provide distinct feedback as to the overall success or failure of the goal as a whole. If you clearly known when you have reached a new milestone, then your goal is measurable.

*A:* The best goals are attainable when all of

your unique challenges are taken into account. No matter your intentions a goal that is unattainable is never a good goal.

*R:* The best goals are realistic which means that not only are they attainable, they can be completed based on the amount of time and effort you are going to be able to put forth on average.

**Timely:** The best goals are those which have a specific, but reasonable, timetable for completion. Goals that are too strict when it comes to a timetable will never come to fruition in time; meanwhile, goals that are too vague when it comes to a timetable will also never see success because it is too easy to put them off indefinitely.

**Keep track of your progress:** Especially when you are new to options trading, you will likely find it useful to keep extremely precise notes when it comes to the trades you made, the mental state you were in when you made them, and the ultimate outcome of each. It is important to keep track of these metrics throughout your day, every day, but to also to avoid pouring over them at the end of each day with the goal of passing judgment on your system. A good system needs at least a few weeks to determine if it is at all worthwhile, and then another 2 weeks if its results are near 50 percent or better. There is nothing to be gained by looking for results where there are none that are strong enough to be accurate seen. Be patient and the information you have to analyze will be much more useful.

**Place your first trade**

Once you have a clear idea of what your plan is going to be, now's the time to put it to the test for the first time. While you can start with practice options, that will only teach you the mechanics, not how to deal with your emotions and the other important mental components required to trade options effectively. As such, it is recommended that you start off will extremely low cost options so you have learned by doing.

**Find the right online broker for you**: Unlike the old days, new options traders have plenty of different options when it comes to choosing an online brokerage, which you will need to do before you can make your first trade. When looking for an online brokerage that is right for you, you first need to ask yourself what unique needs, if any, you have when it comes to a brokerage, as well as their rules regarding fees, number of positions allowed per order and more. When you are first getting started, however, it is best to stick with one that is as user friendly as possible. For the purposes of this walkthrough, it will be assumed that you choose TradeKing.com.

Trade King offers a starter package that makes them a good choice for new options traders for several reasons. First of all, their commission structure is nice and simple as well as extremely competitive so you will always know what it is you are on the hook for with every trade. There is a $4.95 fee for each trade that you make through their platform as well as an additional 65 cents charged for each option that is part of the trade. Additionally, you will need to pay $9.95 in order to exercise options and $4.95 to exercise options. What's more, there is no minimum deposit so you can get started at any level with which you feel comfortable.

### Make a trade

When it comes time to make your first trade you will first want to login to your TradeKing account before choosing the Trading option and then the option to Trade Options.

Next you will be taken to a page where you will be able to see current price quotes for any stock that you can think of as long as you know their related ticker symbol. For example, type in AAPL to pull up the current price of Apple stock.

After that you will start seeing a stream of quotes on various options related to AAPL as well as their underlying stock quotes. For your purposes you should focus on the options.

Next you are going to want to go ahead and determine what month of options you are interested in trading. The *Front Month* is the next month that is going to expire. Go ahead and choose the front month for your first trade.

With a month selected you will then be shown a table that denotes strike prices for calls as well as puts. Find a strike price that looks good to you based on your current evaluation of the market.

You will then want to determine if a call or a put makes the most sense based on the current potential of the market. Once you have found the one that is right for you, you will want to select the option for Ask/Bid Quotes to pull up the order form for the option you have selected. In this instance, it is important to keep in mind that the option to Bid equates to selling an option and Ask equates to buying an option.

On the next menu you are going to determine how many of the option in question you are interested in purchasing. You then are allowed to set the price that you are going to pay for the option. As a new options trader you will also want to stick with Limited order type for now which means that you will only pay the amount you specified.

Finally, you will want to determine how long the order will stay open if it does not get filled. If you choose the Day option, then the order will expire at the end of the day. If you choose the longer, GTC option then the order will not expire until you cancel it.

Finally, all that is left to do is to confirm that you are willing to make the trade that you have arranged. Before you click the send button to confirm your order it is important that you take a few extra moments to double check that everything is as you want it. This small step can save you big time in the long run.

Hit send and you are done!

# Chapter 5

# STRATEGIES

# TO CONSIDER

Becoming a successful options trading means taking in an extremely large amount of information at an extremely high rate of speed. Luckily, there are plenty of simple strategies that can be used to identify the right trades at the right times. Before you begin using any of these strategies it is important to have a clear idea of what their indicators are and how you can best put them to work for you. Just because you have a strategy that will work in certain circumstances, doesn't mean you have the plan to go ahead and use it properly.

*Covered Call:* To implement a covered call, you start by investing in the underlying stock of an option you have identified while simultaneously generating a call related to that same stock. This strategy will only work if you create a call for the exact amount related to the amount of the underlying stock you purchased. This is an ideal strategy to use if you are looking to compliment an existing short-term strategy or feel that the stock in question is going to remain neutral throughout the length of the option.

For example, assuming you buy 100 shares of a company for $38 per and then sell calls at $40 for $1. This way you will bring in $100 from what you have sold which essentially cuts the total cost of the stock to $37. Therefore, if the expiration of the calls arrives and the stock price is at $40 or less, then the calls will expire and you will retain the premium.

**Married Put:** If you own a number of shares of a potential volatile stock that you are keen to hold on to in hopes of future profits, you best course of action is to perform what is known as a married put. Essentially, you buy a put for the total amount of your existing shares and hedge your bet when it comes to minimizing potential losses.

For example, if you buy 100 shares of a company at $20 a share, and one put valued at $17.50 in the front month for 50 cents per share ($50 total). In so doing you create insurance on the price of the shares you purchased.

**Bull Call Spread:** To properly utilize this strategy you will first want to call an option that you have your eye one at a profitable strike price before then selling the same number of calls a strike price that is higher still. These calls should be related to the same underlying stock and have the same timeframe. This is a great choice if you have reason to believe that the underlying stock price is going to move in a positive direction during the option's timeframe.

This type of spread is also often referred to as a vertical credit spread due to its pair of legs. One of the legs is longer than the other, the leg that you hold on to even if the price continues to rise. This creases what is known as a *credit spread* which is known to contain a net profit as well as minimizing the decay related to time value. If one of the options turns out to be a short option, then it is considered a *debit spread* instead which makes it a bad choice instead of a good one.

For example, if you find a company that is currently trading around $37.50 and is expected to trade as high as $49 in the next month. For a bear call spread you would buy 5 call options at $38 that are trading at $1 and expire in 30 days; while, at the same time, selling 5 call options at $39 for 50 cents per and expiring in the same time frame. Because each option is worth 100 shares the math works out to be $500 for the 500 $1 shares minus $250 for the 500 50 cent shares which results in a $250 profit minus commission fees which are not included.

**Bear Put Spread:** Like the Bull Call Spread, the Bear Put Spread is a type of vertical spread, though it is one that is useful in precisely the opposite scenario. Specifically, you would start by purchasing put options at a beneficial strike price before selling the same amount at a point that is lower still while keeping everything else about them the same. This is the right choice when you feel the value of the underlying stock will be decreasing and you want to limit your loses if things don't go according to your plan. Unfortunately, this also limits your potential profits as you can never make more than the difference between the two strike points minus any applicable fees.

This means that the ideal time to use a Bear Put Spread is when you are already planning on short selling a certain stock and using a traditional put option won't suit your needs. They are used most successfully when lowering prices seems like the ideal course of action and you want to hope for the best and still plan for the worst.

For example, if you find a company that is currently trading around $100 and is expected to trade as high as $103 in the next month. For a bear put spread you would want to write 3 put options for $100 each that trade for $3 and expire in 30 days; while, at the same time, buying 3 put options at $97 that trade for $1 and expire in 30 days. Therefore, you have $900 wrapped up in the first trade and $300 in the other which means that assuming the second trade loses money you will still make $600 minus commissions which are not included.

**Protective Collar:** A protective collar strategy is put into action when you buy a put option that is not currently profitable while writing a separate call option that is also not currently profitable that has the same underlying stock. This is often used when you have previously taken a long position on the underlying stock in question which has currently seen numerous, significant, gains. This will ensure you are able to keep a steady level of profit while still keeping a set number of shares to hedge against future profits.

Creating a protective collar is done by placing a put order related to the underlying stock in question while choosing a strike price that makes you a significant return on your initial investment. You then complete the collar strategy by writing a related call on the same underlying stock which means your profits are ensured in case things take a dramatic or unexpected turn.

For example, if you look at a company which closed at $109.25 today, which you initially purchased 100 shares in when it was worth just $70. To protect your current profits, you start by creating a covered call, say at $115 which costs $3.65. You would then write an option related to the underlying stock to then create $365 in profit before commissions are taken into account. Additionally, you would then want to but a $105 put option that trades at $4.50 which would cost $450. This means you would then pay a net total of $85 to protect your initial gains.

**Long Straddle:** This is a strategy to use after you have already purchased a put option in addition to a call option and both use the same underlying stock, date of expiration and even strike price. This is a useful strategy if you are sure the price of the underlying stock is going to shift substantially, but you are not sure what type of shift it is going to be. This means you are going to be in the best possible position to see the profits you are hoping for one way or the other, it will only cost you double the usual rate of fees because either way you are going to be walking away from an unfulfilled option.

For example, if you buy a put option and also a call option with a strike price of $50 while the underlying stock is also work $50 and there are 2 months left until both options expire and they are both currently going for $2. To execute a long straddle, you would start by paying $400 ($200 per option). This will limit the amount you can possibly lose to just $400 and that is only if there is no movement in the stock price for the next 2 months.

**Short Straddle**: A short straddle is the opposite of a long straddle which means you instead sell a pair of calls that have the same underlying stock, expiration date and total amount. This guarantees you are going to see a profit as long as the market doesn't move very much in the interim. If the market decides to pick a direction, however, then your profit margin in these scenarios is likely to evaporate extremely quickly.

For example, if there is a certain stock that is trading for $40 in the month of June, then in order to create a short straddle you would want to sell a $40 put for the month of July for a total of $200 while at the same time selling a $40 call for $200. This will ensure that you make a maximum of $400 for the trade but also minimize the total amount of your potential losses.

## Chapter 6

## ANALYZING YOUR RESULTS

As was previously mentioned, while you might be tempted to set daily trading goal totals for yourself, this will only lead to an influx of negative trading behaviors that will only cause you more harm than good in the long run. You should still make it a point to take detailed notes, however, which means you will want to make a note of all of the relevant metrics discussed above and how the trade ultimately worked out. Having this data will ultimately help you determine if the plan you have created is going to be effective in the long term.

The metrics that you are likely going to find the most useful will vary based on personal trading style and will tend to be focused more around the total amount of profit you have earned so far or how high your successful trade percentage is. If you have a higher amount of acceptable risk, then you will likely want to consider your total profit amount and if you are prioritizing consistency over general profits then percentage of trades successful is a better metric for success.

**Create a performance report**

You will use the data you have record to create a performance report relating to the trading plan or strategy that you are currently using. This report will let you take a critical look at the rules you are using the determine your trades and determine how it is likely going to continue performing over a set period of time. Creating a performance report will help you understand the historical volatility of your plan.

When getting started with a performance report, the best place to start is by creating a summary of the metrics that you have collected over the past few weeks. Ideally you will want to include information on every trade that was completed, if it was a put or a call, the time and data it occurred and the results of the trade overall. While it will be tempting, you will find that avoiding daily data will make it easier to see the forest for the trees.

Keeping a broader focus will help you determine not just the amount you are making overall but also why certain trades failed while others succeeded. Taking the time to do so can make it easier for you to turn fluke instances of success into patterns instead. When it comes to determining your performance you are also going to want to check in on your performance graph which can be found under Tools on the TradeKing site. This graph can either be seen as a bar graph or as what is known as an equity curve, though the bar graph will be illustrative enough to immediately tell you what you need to know.

## Results to focus on

When it comes to sorting through all of the data that is available to you, you will find it easier to focus of a few major indicators and then let the rest fall in line as expected.

*Total net profit:* When it comes to determining your total net profit, you are looking to determine at the highest possible level if the plan or strategy that you were using was a success or failure because it determines whether or not you made more money than you lost. To find this number you simply take your total amount of gains and subtract from that the total amount you lost while also taking into account commission costs and any other relevant fees. This will tell you if you are on the right course or if you need to scrap everything and start fresh.

**Profit factor:** Once your total net profit is facing the right way, the next thing you are going to need to consider how much you are likely to make on your plan per dollar spent assuming everything else remains equal. To find this number you simple take your total profit number and divide it by the total amount of any losses you had. This number needs to be above 1 in order to indicate a profitable plan and anything higher is extremely profitable.

**Percent profitable:** You can think of the percent your plan is profitable as how likely you are to win at any given trade. To determine what the number is you simply take the number of trades that ended in success and divide it by the total number of trades that you attempted. There is no target number in this scenario, as the right number depends on whether you prefer major gains and higher risks, in which case you should aim for few trades with higher margins; or you will want a high number if you prefer lots of small, safe trades.

**Trade average net profit:** The trade average net profit is the amount you are likely to make on each trade you complete, given your past history of trading. To find this number all you need to do is divide the total amount of profit you made by the total number of trades, regardless of whether or not they were ultimately successful. This number should be positive, and ideally, the higher the better.

If the number ends up being negative, then you need to stop trading until you come up with a plan that is somewhat more effective. When finding this number, it is important to leave out any trades that you may have made that were extreme outliers compared to all of your other trades as they can skew this number to the point of irrelevance.

## Chapter 7

## TIPS FOR SUCCESS

*Stay away from calls that are Out of the Money:* If a call is not at least at the money then it is not worth your time. While you have likely heard the old adage, buy low and sell high, that is never the right choice in this case as calls that are out of the money are much less likely to get back to where they need to be if you hope to turn a profit on them. This, in turn, amounts to little more than gambling because there are always going to be relatively few indicators that you can rely on to determine if the price is going to stabilize in the time allotted.

It is important to keep in mind that buying an option means knowing what direction an underlying stock is going to move in, but it is just as important to know when it is going to move in that direction. If you misjudge either, then you are likely to lose out on the commission in addition to not being able to use that money in other more profitable ways until the option expires. Don't forget, in order to make money you need the option to increase all the way from out of the money to the strike price if you want to make a profit.

**Work out multiple strategies:** Eventually you will start to feel constrained by the system or plan that you are utilizing and want to expand into a wider variety of options. When this happens it is important that you work out new plans and strategies instead of trying to force your existing strategy to work in ways that it was not designed to. Certain strategies are always only going to work in certain scenarios and trying to force them to do otherwise is just asking for trouble. What's worse, these faulty decisions are going to taint your overall trade average, making your plan seem worse than it actually is.

*Utilize a spread:* A long spread is comprised of a pair of options, one with a higher cost and the other with a lower cost. The higher cost option is the one that you will buy and the other is the one that you will sell. Everything about the pair of options should be the same except for their strike prices. When using a spread, it is important that you always keep the time value in mind less you find yourself in a scenario where it serves to limit your profits.

**Always be clear on when you will be entering or exiting:** Ensuring that you know exactly when you want to start a trade or to exit an existing trade can become more difficult the more your emotions begin to come into play. While it will be difficult to leave money on the table at first, having limits to your trade will keep you from losing much more money than it will ultimately cost you. What's more, when you think about the amount of money that you are likely to gain in the short period between when you should exit a trade and when you ultimately do, the amount saved is typically going to be negligible.

**Don't double up:** If a trade that appears as though it is going to turn a profit suddenly and unexpectedly moves in the wrong direction, the reaction of many novice options traders is going to be let emotion get the better of you and possibly double down on what is rapidly becoming a bad investment in hopes of making back all of the money that was previously lost. If you find yourself in a situation where you are thinking about doubling down on something questionable you can keep yourself from making the wrong decision by first asking yourself if you would have made the decision if things had gone your way from the start. In nearly all scenarios, cutting your losses and moving forward with a clear head is the preferable action. Remember, there are always more profitable trades on the horizon.

**Keep earnings dates in mind:** When it comes to maximizing your earnings potential it is important to have a clear idea of when any of the underlying stocks related to your options are going to have to disclose their earnings for the past quarter. Regardless of what the outcome of these calls is going to be, they are sure to generate a fair amount of movement when it comes to the stock in question which means being caught unaware can leave you trading based on information that is suddenly extremely outdated. Option prices typically tend to spike around earnings time as a result.

Additionally, it is important to keep in mind when any underlying stock is going to be paying dividends as well. This is extremely important because unless you exercise the options related to the stocks that are going to be paying dividends then you won't make any money in the process. These dividends can sometimes be assigned earlier than expected which is why you always want to have a firm grasp on the newest information available regarding the dates in question.

**Understand the risk of early assignment:** It is common for new traders to sell options or months without realizing they are putting themselves at risk until they are handed their first early assignment and are forced to deal with it in any way possible. Early assignment occurs when a holder exercises their rights well before the expiration date of the option in question that you are the writer on and it means you have to fulfill your obligation even if the terms aren't as much in your favor as you would like. If this happens to you the best thing you can do is not to let your emotions get the better of you and instead look for ways to make the best of a bad situation before committing to anything specific.

**Commit to spreads only when appropriate:** When you are first starting out it can be easy to start a spread, consider all available options and then setting up the remainder of the spread. If you typically find yourself buying a call, finding the best possible moment, and then setting up a sell call then you will likely find yourself in a situation where a sudden change of fortune between the two makes seeing even a marginal return on your investment more difficult than you previously intended. This can easily be presented by committing to a spread all at once as this will provide fewer chances for various variables to sneak in and ruin your calculations.

**Trade what you can afford to lose**: One of the most difficult lessons for many new options traders to learn is that you must never put more into a trade than you can realistically afford to lose, regardless of how good of a deal the trade appears to be at the time. There is never, ever going to be a trade that is a sure thing which means that luck will always play a factor no matter how air tight your system may have appeared to be in the past. If you typically take bigger risks than you can realistically afford, it isn't a question of if you will learn your lesson, it is a matter of when.

**CONCLUSION**

Thank for making it through to the end of *Options Trading: Options Trading for Beginners*, let's hope it was informative and able to provide you with all of the tools you need to achieve your goals both in the near term and for the months and years ahead. Remember, just because you've finished this book doesn't mean there is nothing left to learn on the topic. Becoming an expert at something is a marathon, not a sprint, slow and steady wins the race.

The next step is to stop reading already and to start putting together the type of options trading plan that makes the most sense for you. While you may want to hurry up and jump in, restrain yourself, because what you are going to want to do first is research, and lots of it. While it may seem tedious, attempting to utilize options training without doing your research is akin to gambling; and if you are interested in gambling, you can find much better rates of return in ways that require much less effort than options trading. Do your homework and reap the rewards, it is as simple as that.

## Options Trading FAQ's

- **What are the benefits of trading options?**

    1. Options offer great leverage. You are able to control 100 shares of stock for a few hundred dollars or less.

    - 2. Options can allow us to make money in many types of market conditions. Even then stocks are moving sideways.

    - 3. There are options trades that can allows us to make money 5 different ways.

    - 4. Trading options can be done in as little as

10 minutes a day.

- 5. Options trading allows us to control our risk better than any other financial instrument out There

  - **What options broker is best to use?**

  While there are many options brokers available these days, there are two that we recommend above the rest. The first is TastyWorks (https://www.tastyworks.com) and TD Ameritrade (https://www.tdameritrade.com). Both of these brokers offer great platforms with low commission rates. For those of you with busy schedules that like to trade from a mobile platform, both of these brokers also provide mobile apps to trade from. The benefit of TastyWorks is they offer a flat $1 per contract commission for an options trade. They also don't charge a closing commission so you will only be paying to enter the trade. They also cap their commissions at $10 per trade ($10 per leg on a spread). This can lead to big savings if you are trading bigger position sizes. Finally, TastyWorks doesn't have different levels of accounts like most other brokers. If you open an account with them you can trade any options strategy you want (long calls and puts as well as spreads). For these reasons, TastyWorks is our broker of choice.

**Should I open a margin or cash account?** We prefer using a margin account as it will allow us to trade vertical spreads. While you can open a cash account with less capital, you will be limited to buying calls and puts. This will greatly limit your flexibility in different market conditions. Most brokers require a

$3,000 starting account size to open a margin account. Cash accounts can be opened with as little as $50.

**What is the pattern day trading rule (PDT) and who does it apply to?** Margin accounts under $25,000 are subject to the pattern day trading rule. This rule limits the number of day trades you can take. You are allowed 3 day trades in a 5 day stretch. Cash accounts are not subject to this rule. If you plan on day trading options with an account size less than $25,000 you will be better off with a cash account. How much capital should I start trading with? We recommend starting with a minimum of $3,500. While you can start with less than this it becomes much more difficult to control the risk if you do. Ideally, we want the risk to be kept to 2-5%

of your account per trade.

**Should I day trade or swing trade options?** We find it much easier to swing trade options. We classify a swing trade as holding a position for anywhere from 2 days on out to 3 weeks. Day trading options can be difficult as it takes more time on a daily basis and also becomes less forgiving if the stock doesn't move in your favor immediately.

**Which options strategy is best?** The beauty of options trading is the flexibility that they offer as they allow us to do things that can't be done with any other financial instrument. The 3 strategies that we recommend all options traders use are: • long calls and puts • debit spreads • credit spreads We cover these strategies in detail including step by step criteria for each trade type in the free Options Trading For Income Crash Course which you will find links to above.

**Is volume or open interest more important when trading options?** Liquidity is a very important topic when trading options. The more active the options are the easier it will be to get filled on trades and at good prices. Volume indicates the number of contracts traded that day. Open interest will tell you the total number of option contracts that are outstanding. These are contracts that have been traded but have not been closed by an offsetting trade or an exercise or assignment. Unlike trading volume, open interest is not updated during the trading day. Ideally, we like to see good volume and open interest in the options that we trade.

However, open interest is more important to us as it indicates those options have been active over a period of days. This will typically lead to tighter bid/ask spreads on the options, which means we will be able to get in and out of our trades at better prices.

**Are weekly or monthly options best to trade?** We prefer to use options that have between 20-60 days left to expiration. This could be a mix of weekly options that have at least 20 days left to expiration along with monthly options. We find the monthly options easier to trade in most cases as they will have better liquidity meaning the volume and open interest are higher. We are open to trading the shorter duration options but like to see the VIX in the upper teens or low twenties

when doing so.

**Should I trade In the Money or Out Of The Money options?** While the out of the money options are attractive due to being cheaper, we much prefer trading the in the money options. They provide a higher quality position which will increase your odds of success. The out of the money options are cheap for a reason because they have a lower probability of success as there are more factors working against them. When buying options, we prefer to buy the options that are 1-2 strikes in the money from the entry point on your chart. This will give us the most bang for our buck. Stock movement vs Implied volatility vs Time decay All 3 of these can have a big impact on the prices of an option. When buying options, you need a big enough directional move in the stock in your favor and it has to happen quickly enough to offset the time decay and potential movement in volatility. I'm not opposed to buying options, but you need a lot to go right in your favor to make money. If the stock doesn't move fast enough or volatility drops too much while you are in the trade, you won't be as profitable. Trading credit spreads allows you to put on a trade where you are benefiting from time decay adding up and volatility decreasing. You are able to stack the deck in your favor by placing a trade that has 5 ways of making money. Stock movement, implied volatility, and time decay are all crucial factors to take into consideration when placing an options trade. Ignoring one of these factors can lead to very inconsistent returns over time. We talk about this in more detail in our free

Options Trading For Income Crash Course at the links to above. Should,

**I use limit or market orders when placing my trades?** We highly recommend using limit orders when placing your options trades. When you use market orders you lose control over where you get filled at. This can lead to giving up too much on the fill prices. Market orders should only be used as a last resort option. When using limit orders, we like to place the orders at the mid price between the bid and ask prices. While this doesn't guarantee you will get filled on a trade at these prices, it's a good place to start. If you are placing a buy order and can't get filled at the mid price then you can adjust the order price higher by a few pennies. If you are placing a sell order and can't get filled at the mid price then you can adjust the order price lower by a few pennies. Doing so will increase your odds of getting filled.

CPSIA information can be obtained
at www.ICGtesting.com
Printed in the USA
BVHW091149260722
643030BV00003B/288